My C Book

by Jane Belk Moncure
illustrated by Linda Hohag

THE CHILD'S WORLD

ELGIN, ILLINOIS 60120

Library of Congress Cataloging in Publication Data

Moncure, Jane Belk.
  My "c" book.

  (My first steps to reading)
  Rev. ed. of: My c sound box. © 1979.
  Summary: Little c fills her box with a variety of
things that begin with a hard "c."
  1. Children's stories, American.   [1. Alphabet]
I. Hohag, Linda. ill.   II. Moncure, Jane Belk.   My
c sound box.   III. Title.   IV. Series: Moncure, Jane
Belk.   My first steps to reading.
PZ7.M739Myc   1984   [E]   84-17534
ISBN 0-89565-278-1

Distributed by Childrens Press, 1224 West Van Buren Street,
Chicago, Illinois 60607.

My "c" Book

(This book uses only the hard "c" sound in the story line. Blends are included. Words beginning with the soft "c" sound and the "ch" sound are included at the end of the book.)

Little c had a  box.

She said, "I will fill my  box."

Little was cold.

She found coats.

Little  put on one coat.

She put two coats into her box.

Little  found caps.

She put on
one cap.

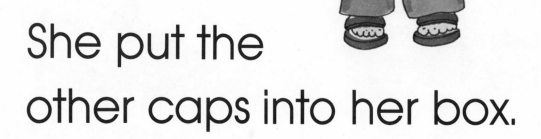

She put the
other caps into her box.

Little  found a caterpillar.

It made a cocoon.

She put the cocoon into her box.

Little  found a car.

Away she went.

She found a cat
and a canary.

Little  said to the cat,
"In you go."

box

14

She found a cage
for the canary.

"In you go, canary," she said.

Little  came to a cornfield.

She found a cow and a calf.

Little 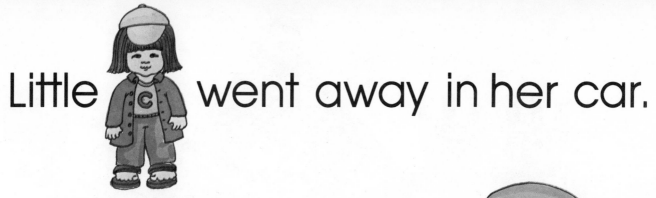 went away in her car.

She found a camel. Then, she...

found a candy castle.

A clown said, "Will you come in?"

Little  said, "Yes."

"Guess what?" said the clown.

"I have  candy canes,

 cookies, and  a cake

with candles on it.

"It is my birthday.
Come to my party."

Little  took off
her coat and cap.

She took her things
out of her box.

She went
to the party.

cage

canary

cow

calf

candy   candy canes

"What a nice birthday party,"

cat

camel

clown

candles

cake

cookies

cocoon

she said.

More words with Little

crown

camera

cup

cotton candy

can

curtain

carrot

comb

cloud

card

3 ♥
♥
♥
♥ ♠
3

crayon

cowboy

calendar

			1	2	3	4
5	6	7	8	9	10	11
12	13	14	15	16	17	18
19	20	21	22	23	24	25
26	27	28	29	30	31	

cape

cucumber

In this story Little  has the sound of the  letter "k."

Little  has another sound — the sound of the letter "s."

Read these Little  words.

circle

centipede

cigar

cent

celery

cymbals

cereal

city

29

Little  gets together with the letter "h" for another sound

chalkboard

chalk

cherry

chain

church

chocolate

chicken

chimney

chipmunk